J.S.C. McLaren.

Jan. 1960.

£4-00

46/23

MIRACLE AT MIDNIGHT

MIRACLE AT MIDNIGHT

A play with Carols for Christmas

by

TOM FLEMING

LONDON : THE EPWORTH PRESS

THE EPWORTH PRESS
(FRANK H. CUMBERS)
25-35 City Road, London, E.C.1

MELBOURNE   CAPE TOWN
NEW YORK   TORONTO

SET IN MONOTYPE GARAMOND AND PRINTED IN
GREAT BRITAIN BY THE CAMELOT PRESS LTD.,
LONDON AND SOUTHAMPTON

Miracle at Midnight was first presented at the Gateway Theatre, Edinburgh, on the 22nd December 1952, with the following cast:

The Players

A Herd	DOUGLAS STORM
A Snowman	GEORGE DAVIES
A Man	JOHN YOUNG
A Displaced Person . . .	NORA LAIDLAW
A Mother	LENNOX MILNE
Mary, the Mother of Christ .	MARGARET REID

The Singers

FENELLA BALDWIN

CONSTANCE MULLAY

DUNCAN ROBERTSON

FREDERICK WESTCOTT

The play was produced by the Author.

FOR MY FRIENDS AND COLLEAGUES
AT THE GATEWAY THEATRE, EDINBURGH,
WHO WITH SUCH DEEP SINCERITY
FIRST BROUGHT THESE LINES TO LIFE
TO THE GLORY OF ALMIGHTY GOD

(*The action of the play is continuous and takes place within one setting which remains throughout. The essential impression of the whole is that of a vivid Christmas-card scene with which is intermingled something of the mystical, something of the real. There are two levels—stage level, and a raised level consisting of two rostra placed symmetrically right and left. Upon each rostrum is a bench such as might be found in any public park, lit by a single lamp-post. Here, it may be, is the world of that elusive norm—the 'man-in-the-street'. Centre stage between the rostra is a tall fabrication, of no definitive style, to the timbered roof of which cling long fingers of snow. Perhaps the suggestion of a stable is there when one looks at it more closely, but nothing more. From the front wall of this centrepiece there is cut out, at a height which dominates the entire stage, a silver star. Until the moment of miracle, this has significance only as the star upon the Christmas tree placed centre stage directly beneath it. Around this tree and upon its branches are Christmas gifts wrapped in many gay and varied colours, and among these there may clearly be seen a toy donkey, a doll's house, a silk kerchief, and an enormous white stocking. Steps lead from each rostrum to stage level, and down right is the immobile bulk of the Snowman. Against the sky-cloth which backs the set are silhouetted the incongruous and angular shapes of a contemporary sky-line. A factory chimney, a tenement roof-top, a church tower and sundry telegraph poles and pylons merge in a harsh, repetitive pattern of reality.*)

The Curtain rises on a darkened stage. From the darkness comes the soft music of a shepherd's pipe playing an indeterminate tune that is filled at once with a great longing and a tenderly persistent appeal. Slowly we can distinguish the figure of a young herd. He is dressed in a rough goatskin, and it is as if he sat there for ever playing to the night sky his simple theme. Suddenly he stops, and appears to be listening. . . . But after a moment he starts to play again, and as his plaintive little melody ends we are aware of a distant singing—ethereal, wordless singing that swells and fades. He smiles as he hears it, looks about him as though the voices were now here, now there, until they linger away out of hearing. There is a moment's silence. . . . Then he speaks:

9

Every eve of every year
Alone
And unattended by the world
I sit here.
Sit upon this upland waste of Time
Piping a tune to the singing-silvered spheres:
The theme Eternal—
Of a Will and Purpose
Over and above all things;
Above all, good;
The theme Eternal
Born into flesh and blood,
Conceived above,
Born into agony and love.

(The singing is heard again slightly farther off.)

I was a shepherd once—
A boy that sat upon a hillside
Keeping sheep,
Watching them sleep,
Piping a tune,
Wide-eyed,
To while away the lingering hours
That crept by
With a hungering cry
Of terror in the night.
I think I had a name once;
A long forgotten name—
So long
Forgotten,
A score of infinite eternities ago!
Long—
Like some never-waking day-dream. . . .
Yet sometimes it can seem
Like only yesterday
I sat—

A boy upon a hillside
Keeping sheep,
Watching them sleep,
Piping a tune—
And yesterday I saw a star
Rise in the midnight sky,
Dimly in the distance
Heard cattle groan,
In labour not their own;
Heard away above the moon-kissed fields
A singing
As of angels bringing
Tidings of great joy:
The great Creator come upon the Earth
A creature,
Fashioned in the image of His own unceasing Love.
My brothers heard it too,
Left their sheep, followed the star
Where far
Across the rolling plain it beckoned.
I stayed behind—
Someone had to keep a watch
Against the swift-foot howling
Prowling
In the dark. . . .

How could I have reckoned
Staying behind
I'd lose the coming of the Son of God?
Forfeit
For a flock of ragged dirty sheep
My homage to the infant King of Kings, asleep?

Now every eve of every year
I sit here—
Sitting out Eternity
To point the way that Star, undimmed, is leading,
Pipe my tune of endless, ageless pleading,

Cry in men's hearts
The birthday of their God.
They seldom hear.
All through the year
Their old world bundles on,
Trundles, oblivious, to its own oblivion.
The silver singing of the spheres is drowned
By war-cries,
And bloodshot eyes
Seek out their vaulted treasure in the ground.
But once a year
Through all the din,—
The pile-driven pillory of man's habitual Sin,
My shepherd's pipe is heard,
I play my little tune
And the theme Eternal
Thrills
Through the silence of a split-soul Universe.
Hearts beat faster,
Kindliness loiters unmolested at the crossways of the
    world,
A moment of magic
In one fleeting fragmentary fleck of Time.

Look up, world!
Lift your heavy heart to the star-spun sky!
Tonight I cry
The Birthday of your God!
Tonight
The Light of Light
Is come upon the Earth.
Be glad!
Turn aside from days
Of heartache on the withered ways,
For it is Christmas:
CHRISTMAS   CHRISTMAS   CHRISTMAS!

(As he speaks the word 'Christmas' these three times the lighting

spots in turn the SNOWMAN, *the* CHRISTMAS TREE, *and the* SINGERS *who stand grouped beneath the lamp-post on the rostrum up left. They are dressed in scarlet cassocks with white collars, and sing together this merry Yuletide carol):*

> Wassail, Wassail, all over the town!
> Our toast it is white, and our ale it is brown,
> Our bowl it is made of the white maple tree;
> With the wassailing bowl we'll drink to thee.
>
> So here is to Cherry and to his right cheek,
> Pray God send our master a piece of good beef,
> And a good piece of beef that may we all see;
> With the wassailing bowl we'll drink to thee.
>
> And here is to Dobbin and to his right eye,
> Pray God send our master a good Christmas pie,
> And a good Christmas pie that may we all see;
> With our wassailing bowl we'll drink to thee.
>
> So here is to Broad May and to her broad horn,
> May God send our master a good crop of corn,
> And a good crop of corn that may we all see;
> With the wassailing bowl we'll drink to thee.
>
> Then here's to the maid in the lily white smock,
> Who tripped to the door and slipped back the lock,
> Who tripped to the door and pulled back the pin,
> For to let these jolly wassailers in.

> *Gloucestershire Wassail: traditional*

(They are still singing as they leave the stage and we see that beside the SNOWMAN *an ordinary* MAN *is standing. He is a* MAN *of the city business vintage, wears a dark jacket, striped trousers, stiff white collar and bowler hat, and he carries a brief case, a folded umbrella, and a daily newspaper. The situation is made slightly comic by the fact that the* SNOWMAN *beside him also wears a bowler—in his case a somewhat battered and ill-fitting adornment!)*

SNOWMAN

(Desperately keen to make conversation)

Aye, a fine bit song. . . .
Bonny cheery voices too. . . .
Cauld though the night. . . .
D'ye no think?
To tell you the truth
I dinna very often think mysel'.
Snell
Wind souchin' aff the Arctic Sea—
Mind, healthy weather
For the likes o' me. . . .
Eh . . . Waitin' on someone, sir?

MAN

Doing a crossword . . .
Standing in a queue . . .
And you?

SNOWMAN

Human!
Eh, me?
Oh, I'm queued up an' a',
Waitin' like yoursel'
For better days, an' syne
The thaw.
Been here since I was born—
Yesterday that was,
An' like as no I'll still be here
The morn. . . .
Unless . . .
Och! but Jockie Frost'll see me richt
For yet a while.

MAN

Has the midnight gone?

SNOWMAN

To tell the truth
I never was a chap for clocks.
Never hae muckle need o' them—
Or bedsocks! !

MAN

LATE!

SNOWMAN

Or early,
Late or early, never need them,
Never.

MAN

You've been here
Since yesterday. It can't
Have gone.

(*The* HERD *has appeared in the darkness.*)

HERD

What are you waiting for?

MAN

The midnight. This chap's
Been there since yesterday
Or the one before!
It really is

15

The limit. That he should stand
For days. . . .
Twenty-four-man-hour days
Doing nothing
In a snowfield!
Think what it means!

SNOWMAN

A lifetime. . . .

MAN

A lifetime wasted.
This pillar of potential productivity
Forced by a circumstance
Beyond his own control
To be an idle gossip.
Sheer
Muddle-headed inefficiency!
There must be a Society
For the Intention
Of such Midnight Redundancy.
We'll seek them out
The dilatory engineers of idleness!
We'll not stand this—
Eh, fellow?

SNOWMAN

To tell the truth, Sir,
Standin's aa I'm muckle
Guid for. . . .

MAN

Who do they think they are?
Huh, tell me that!

HERD

Who do you think you are?

MAN

To tell the truth . . . tcha!
You've got *me* at it now. . . .

HERD

The truth
You do not know
You would find hard to tell—
To tell the truth
You are the world.

MAN

Never been as late as this
Before.

He looks at his watch, takes out a cigarette and lights it.

HERD

The world in all its tragedy.

MAN

This midnight lurker in the goatskin
Thinks the world of me!

SNOWMAN

Eh, . . . sir. . . .
The match. . . .
If you'll forgive me,
Matches

Arena unco guid
For me. Heat my bluid,
Ye ken.
Undermine my constitution.

MAN

Oh . . . really?
We must put a question to the House.
Why are matches detrimental
To the health of . . .
What was your occupation
Did you say?

SNOWMAN

I *didn't* say, sir. . . .
To tell the truth . . .

MAN

Ah! yes . . . of course. . . . (*He writes on a scrap of paper*)
'The health of tellers of the Truth'—
Interesting point,
We must further investigate
At a higher level.
The modern state,
The social and industrial evolution
Of mankind,
Can never tolerate
The undermining of one single constitution.
A match. . . .
How odd . . . well, well.

HERD

Beware the world that says, 'To Hell
With Truth'.

18

SNOWMAN

Hell!
Losh!
Dinna mention that word
Within a mile o' me.
The very soond o't
Maks a dreep begin
Coursin' doon my chin.
Truth an' Snawmen
Wad hae but short shrift there!

HERD

Scarce shorter than the shrift
They both find in the world.

MAN

What's all this talk of worlds?
Some shaggy dog messed up
The new cosmology?
What of the world?
What world
For Heaven's sake?

HERD

The world you are.
The world in all its tragedy,
The world that has grown up
Too quickly,
Forgotten how to laugh,
Finds playing with its toys
The hardest work of all.
It is
For Heaven's sake I'm here,
You're right. For Heaven's sake
And yours
This talk of worlds.

MAN

Oh come!
All work and no play. . . .
I'm no dull boy,
Take my recreation very seriously.
Most important
The full employment of one's leisure.

HERD

Enjoyment doesn't matter!

MAN

Eh? No,
Nothing . . . like . . . a . . . GAME.

(*He does a dummy drive-off using his umbrella as a golf club.*)

Damnation! Topped it. . . .

(*Looks for his ball in some imaginary 'rough'.*)

SNOWMAN

Clean through the air!
Eh . . . Your ball, sir?
Juist there.

(*He points to a spot just behind the* MAN *who gives him a withering look. The subject is quickly changed!*)

MAN

(*To the* HERD)

What did you mean:
Grown up too quickly?

HERD

You in your office,
Sitting behind your myriad desks;
In your planning room
Plotting
A more luxurious doom
For all and sundry;
With gears and gadgets
In your factories,
With strange test-tube
Elixirs
Splitting atoms over coffee;
The orgy of bumptious bustling,
The arrogance,
The grumble of grey-headed
Aches
Under your bowler.
In short you are the world
In its prime,
Grown old before its time.
That's what I mean.

MAN

Phew!
Send for a soap-box.
You'd be a useful sort of cove
In the Party.
Now look, I've got to work,
Let's face it.
We're bread-and-butter boys
Working for a living.
Giving
Our energy and genius
To the grave problem of existence.
And after all,
I've got to live—
That's what *I* mean.

Living
Was once a birthright
Of the world,
And work a playmate
Of Creation.
But now that living's to be worked for,
Fought for. . . . Yes, even died for. . . .
Since it's become a draught
To be drawn to a drip,
Drained to the dregs,
Exploited to the full, it's scarcely
Worth the bother.
LOVING's the thing the busy world
Was made for—
The unsolicited gift
Sent you by your Maker.

MAN

It's hard to love unless one lives. . . .
And there's precious little time for living
These days.

HERD

Never has the world had so much time
And done so little with it.
What do you do with all your time?
Save it. . . .
Save it for a rainy day—
And when the rain comes. . . .
Use an umbrella.

MAN

I protest.
We use time in a hundred ways.

HERD

To jet-propel yourself
Across the seventh sea—
And *back*, of course, in time for tea!

MAN

Speed yes. . . .
But speed with efficiency
That's the recipe for self-sufficiency!
There's so much that's awry
In the Universe!
Creation left so many ends untied!
The World needs time to set it right,
To probe what's left of the Unknown,
Seek after Truth,
Reduce to scale the cause and effect
Of Time itself.

HERD

More time
To brood on time,
And the relentless tick-tock
Of its passing.

MAN

Work *was* the playmate of Creation—
You said yourself.
Well time *is* the *work*mate of the world.
If not . . . the world becomes a worker
Against time.
Before you know it—
It's too late!

And the great big world stops turning.
No, no, world,
Don't deceive yourself.
Time is and always will be
Master
While you turn your back on love,
Look down, not up,
Turn deaf ears
To the singing of the spheres.
Manacled and fettered,
You serve time amid the must and cobwebs,
Behind the barred windows
Of a finicking chronology.
There's no way out—
Except love. And that's too easy.
All the beating against fate,
And the bleating against hate
Gets you nowhere.
Isn't that just where you've got yourself?
Precisely nowhere!

MAN

If this is nowhere . . . somewhere out of time . . .
Where's the midnight I came seeking?
Where's it got to? Do you think
I've missed it?

HERD

That depends on you.
That's why I cried aloud to you
In the beginning. You musn't
Miss it.
To miss this midnight
Is the nearest thing to Hell.

Why don't you ask?—There's
The Enquiry Office.

(*He indicates the* SNOWMAN.)

MAN

Any news of the midnight?

SNOWMAN

They say it's held up:
A thick fog of widespread doubt
Along the line.

MAN

Oh, thanks. I'll wait.
Is this the Waiting Room?

HERD

The waiting room of all the world.
Yes, go in there and wait.
Too many miracles are lost for the want
Of a little waiting. Wait. Warm your heart
At the log-fire lopped from the Tree
Of a Life that is greater than living.
Soon you'll hear that midnight song,
They'll not keep you waiting long. . . .

(*The* MAN *sits by the Christmas tree centre. The* SNOWMAN
becomes once more an inanimate object. The SINGERS *entering from
either side mask the figure of the* MAN *from our sight as they sing*):

It came upon the midnight clear,
    That glorious song of old,
From angels bending near the earth
    To touch their harps of gold:
Peace on the earth, good-will to men,
    From heaven's all-gracious King!
The world in solemn stillness lay
    To hear the angels sing.

Still through the cloven skies they come
  With peaceful wings unfurled;
And still their heavenly music floats
  O'er all the weary world;
Above its sad and lowly plains
  They bend on hovering wing,
And ever o'er its Babel sounds
  The blessèd angels sing.

But with the woes of sin and strife
  The world has suffered long;
Beneath the angel strain have rolled
  Two thousand years of wrong;
And man, at war with man, hears not
  The love song which they bring:
O hush the noise, ye men of strife,
  And hear the angels sing.

And ye, beneath life's crushing load
  Whose forms are bending low,
Who toil along the climbing way
  With painful steps and slow—
Look now! for glad and golden hours
  Come swiftly on the wing:
O rest beside the weary road,
  And hear the angels sing.

For lo! the days are hastening on,
  By prophet bards foretold,
When with the ever-circling years
  Comes round the age of gold,
When peace shall over all the earth
  Its ancient splendours fling,
And the whole world give back the song
  Which now the angels sing.

Edmund Hamilton Sears

(*Again the* SINGERS *as they still sing move slowly from the stage, and from the shadows around the Christmas tree the* MAN *appears. He*

*wears a school-cap now, and carries neither brief-case nor umbrella,
but leads the little toy donkey by a string. His voice, when he speaks,
is different, but in no way unnatural—it has regained something of the
ingenuousness and enthusiasm of youth. He is altogether like someone
who finds again what he thought to be irretrievably lost, and remembers
things which have been long forgotten.)*

MAN

Come on, Neddy. I thought I heard
Someone singing. Did you?
It must be very nearly midnight. . . .
What shall we do?
Ooooooh! . . .
Let's explore. Let's pretend
This is a jungle with wild beasts.
Or some big desert
With nobody else at all
In sight. . . .
Oh, but its rather dark
For playing at that
With nobody else
But you and me, Neddy.
I know!—
We'll both be pirates, or highwaymen,
Or robbers; or I'll be
Daniel in the den,
You can be the lion,
Then,
When you come to eat me up,
I'll be too big a helping
And we'll just make friends instead.
Or wait. . . . I'll be St. George
And you can be the dragon. . . .
No, I want to be the dragon—
Then I can roar and puff out flames
And everybody except you
Will be terrified and run away . . .

27

(He breaks off in terror himself.)

> Oh. . . . What's that? . . . Look, Neddy, over there!
> D'you think perhaps . . . it's a REAL dragon? It might be
> Even a ghost. Or a Dentist. . . .

(He hugs Neddy close to him.)

> Oh, Neddy, sometimes it's not much fun
> Being a boy again.
> When all the games are played,
> There's too much time for being afraid. . . .
> Oh, *I'm* not afraid. Are you?
> When I'm grown up I'll carry a gun
> And life will be one
> Big dragon-hunt after another.
> I'll not can be frightened then.
> A stupid ghost. Who'd be afraid?
> Not me! At least . . . I don't think I would.
> You can go first. You may give it a fright.

(Pushing his toy donkey first he approaches the SNOWMAN *warily.
Then suddenly sees what it is. . . .)*

> Whoa, Neddy.
> It's only a silly old snowman. *(He laughs)*
> Look at his hat—
> Who'd ever wear a thing like that!
> Isn't he funny?
> Neddy,
> I wish sometimes snowmen could speak.
> There's lots that they might want to say.
> I wonder if they
> Hang up their stockings at Christmas.
> Oh . . . perhaps they don't have any stockings.
> I wish *(yawning despite himself)*
> Sometimes, Neddy, that *you*
> Could speak.
> Do you think if I asked Santa Claus
> He could help?
> I wish . . . how I wish . . .

HERD

(*Who has been watching unnoticed for some time*)

Time for bed,
Come on, young scamp.

MAN

Oh, not bed yet,
I'm not tired yet.
Please let me stay.

HERD

It's nearly midnight.
And you know what night this is.

MAN

Yes, I know.

HERD

Come along. It's time. Time for bed.

MAN

Oh, BOTHER time. . . . (*reluctantly obeying*) All right. . . .
I'll come.
Can Neddy come too?

HERD

Yes, Neddy can come.

(*The* MAN *picks up the string of the toy donkey, and as he does so he looks round at the snowman standing quite alone and motionless. There is a quick decision—he runs to the Christmas tree, picks up the huge white stocking, and takes it to the* SNOWMAN *who makes never a move. For a moment he is at a loss to know what to do, then timidly he throws the stocking on the ground beside the* SNOWMAN, *picks up Neddy in his arms, and wearily mounts the rostrum steps. By the end of the bench he kneels to say his prayers.*)

MAN

Happy birthday, God.
Bless me and Neddy.
Keep us safe and
Make us good and holy.

(*He lies on the bench and almost immediately begins to fall asleep.*)

Good-night, Neddy. Sweet dreams. . . .

HERD

Now sleeps the busy world
All happed in peace,
Become
Like to the Prince of Peace
A child again.
Now is the time of little things,
Now are the wise
Made wiser in the ways of simpleness.
In very gentleness
The strong wax stronger,
And the rich find riches far beyond account
In the blessedness of giving.
Now sleeps the world,
And living,—
The worry and the weariness,
All the terror and the torment—
Slips away as in a dream.
Hid from unseeing eyes,
Love brings its treasure to the tiny and the wise.

(There comes to us the sound of singing, so soft and simple the voices might be those of little children. As the lamp above the sleeping MAN *fades almost imperceptibly, so the other lamp shines more clearly and reveals to us now the* SINGERS *who are singing)*:

Away in a manger, no crib for a bed,
The little Lord Jesus laid down His sweet head;
The stars in the bright sky looked down where He lay,
The little Lord Jesus asleep on the hay.

The cattle are lowing, the Baby awakes;
But little Lord Jesus, no crying He makes.
I love Thee, Lord Jesus! look down from the sky,
And stay by my side until morning is nigh.

Be near me, Lord Jesus; I ask Thee to stay
Close by me for ever, and love me, I pray;
Bless all the dear children in Thy tender care,
And fit us for heaven, to live with Thee there.

Anonymous

(As they are singing, there enters the DISPLACED PERSON. *She is a young girl of uncertain age, for she has come to maturity through a torment of spiritual and emotional as well as physical hardship. There is a sadness in her eyes which seems out of place in one so young, and yet that very sadness gives her a strange appeal. She is by no means unattractive, and is dressed in a thick ragged jersey and an old pair of rough trousers. She carries all her possessions in a bundle which she drops to the ground as she pauses to listen to the singing. She lurks in the shadows, and as the* SINGERS *leave the stage she makes to follow them, hoping she will be unnoticed. She has not seen the* HERD *enter behind her.)*

HERD

Stop!

(A cruel white searchlight blinds her, flinging her extenuated shadow across the stage.)

Where are you going?
(*She tries to run, but is held by an unseen force. She struggles.*)

It's no use struggling.
There's no running away. You're held
For questioning.

D.P.

Let me go. . . .
(*She tries to struggle free again.*)

HERD

Where would you go, suppose we let you?
(*She gives up the struggle; her arms drop to her side, and at once the searchlight fades.*)

What would you do? Where would you go?
It is against yourself you struggle.
Just answer my questions. We're only trying
To help.

(*She stands silent, still turned away.*)

Name? Occupation? Date of birth?
Have you any papers?
You'd do well to answer
For your own sake.
Now. . . .
What's your name? Where do you come from?
Remember what I said:
All for your own good.

D.P.

My good?
I've answered you a hundred thousand times
And what's the good?
My good. . . .
What is this good you talk about so glibly?

I haven't seen it.
A hundred thousand times. . . .
Would you have me answer you again?
I had the answers off by heart once. . . .
When I had a heart.
Is it the truth you want—
Or might I just as well
Slip you some gloss-enamelled lie
To spare your feelings?
Name? Occupation?
Sprung from a windcast seed
I have no name
Or if I have, I never knew it;
No country—
Or if I have, they must
Have beat the welcome from the threadbare mat
And left the dust;
No occupation—
Or if I have, it is an endless seeking
For some sane relation
To what goes on around me in the world.
There's my inheritance!

(She throws down the bundle she's been carrying.)

The rest I had to leave behind.
Where am I going? To my death
Like countless others.
That's about the limit to the wandering—
The wondering comes after.
What's death when all is said and done to this?
I've suffered terrors worse than dying—
Death's but spilt milk scarce worth the crying
Over.
To die alone,
Unnamed, unknown,
And unremembered. That's what *we* have to face,
The wanderers without a place
To call our own.

HERD

Have you lost the way
That leads you home? Misplaced it?

D.P.

Had it stolen from me.
They displaced it
With another.
Oh, sir, please let me stay here.
I don't mind the fences.
Any job around the camp will do me,
Don't you see—
It's belonging matters most of all.
You know what night this is—
And there's no room
Anywhere else.
Oh, sir.
Let me stay here.
Give me a home.

HERD

I'll tell you what I'll do. . . .
Give you a name—
The rest is up to you.

D.P.

A number's all that I can claim.

HERD

We'll call *you*
The world as well.
The vagrant world. . . .
Sentenced
In the scheme of things

To stray at large outwith the Universe.
The lonely world
So loved of God that His own Son
Saw fit
To wander it,
Homeless and displaced.
Alas!
It's no dread hate
That stuffs Creation's goose
Before it's cooked:
A pinch of pride,
A sprinkling of greed—
An over-abundance of unintended thoughtlessness.
There are your ingredients for sorrow—
Add seasoning to taste.
We'll let you stay.

(*Exit the* HERD.)

D.P.

Thank you. Just for tonight.
Tomorrow
I'll move on.

(*She picks up her belongings, carries her bundle to a corner of the stage and there sits upon it—quite unaware of the* SNOWMAN *beside her. From far away she hears singing, and a peculiar nostalgia gnaws at her heart as she listens—tears could very readily fill her eyes were she not by now in habitual control of her feelings. She nods off to sleep. Her head droops, then her whole body leans against the massive bulk beside her. Very gently a white arm is raised and the* SNOWMAN *places a hand tenderly upon her head.*)

Still the night, holy the night!
Sleeps the world; hid from sight,
Mary and Joseph in stable bare
Watch o'er the Child beloved and fair,
    Sleeping in heavenly rest.

Still the night, holy the night!
Shepherds first saw the light,
Heard resounding clear and long,
Far and near, the angel-song.
    Christ the Redeemer is here!

Still the night, holy the night!
Son of God, O how bright
Love is smiling from Thy face!
Strikes for us now the hour of grace,
    Saviour, since Thou art born!

Joseph Mohr

(The sudden quiet as the singing ends wakens her. She sits up with a start.)

D.P.

Oh!

SNOWMAN

Hae'in a wee bit dream
Tae yersel'?

D.P.

Yes, I think I must have been—
A day-dream
If one can have
A day-dream in the middle of the night.
I thought I heard voices
Singing forgotten things
Somewhere . . . outside. . . .

SNOWMAN

To tell the truth
I thought I did an' a'.

D.P.

Are you a prisoner too?
Or like me—
A displaced person seeking refuge?

SNOWMAN

I suppose ye micht say
A bit o' both.

D.P.

Is this your home, I mean?

SNOWMAN

Ay . . . or . . .
The only hame I've ever seen.

D.P.

I think it was of home
I would have dreamed
Just now—
If ever I'd had one.
When I heard those voices
It was of home they seemed to sing.
They bring
It all so near.

SNOWMAN

Here!
That's enough o' hame chat!
Lassie, gin ye fill my ears
Wi' mair o' that
Ye'll hae me endin' up in tears. . . .

I'm sorry.
I used to sing once,
But all the words have gone long since.
I wonder where they go
When they're forgotten—
All the words that in the speaking
Mean so much.
The thin air
Must be laden with most tender
Whispered things,
They must be there somewhere
For the finding,
The reminding
Of old heartaches and old joys.

SNOWMAN

I never had whit ye'd ca' a voice.
No. Never much o' a singer.
When I sing they've aa' got tae like it
   or lump it!
No, I'm better blawin'
My ain wee bit trumpet! !

D.P.

I'm glad you're here for company.
When one's been used to none,
The world seems overrun,
With two of us.

(*She rises and looks about her.*)

You been here long?

SNOWMAN

Ay, long—
And short. The long an' the short o't is
That soon you find

Ye dinna mind
One wey or the other.

D.P.

They don't take many chances, do they?
Is it to keep people out
They build these barbed wire walls
Of high ideals?
A timely paradox:
'Put freedom in a cage
To keep it safe.'
You're a hero if you go to die
With a neon-lighted battle-cry
Of freedom on your lips,
Yet,
There are so many freedoms, they forget.
The clear, brown river
Gurgling from a mountain spring,
The mist and rain and snow,
The tiniest bird-on-wing—
They're free enough!
And the pale crumpled petal
That falls unnoticed from a withered stem
Is just as free.
There's freedom living
And there's freedom dead—
There is a GLUT of freedom on the earth.
The dearth
Is of belonging.
It was a world that hop-skip-jumped
To fight for freedom
Took the little freedom that I had,
Plundered my belonging
Till now I belong
Nowhere.
In all the wide wandering wilderness
Of the world

39

There is no room for the world itself. . . .
That's what he said I was—
The officer-in-charge, you heard him!
Sorry to weary *you* with my
Philosophy of life.
Becomes something of a habit
To pass away the day-after-day
Along the road.

SNOWMAN

Och, never heed!
I juist let you burble on.
Tae tell the truth,
Mysel'—
I was a wee thing flummoxed
Yet mind, I think—
No verra often, I micht as weel admit it—
That whit you say seems juist aboot tae hit it
On the heid.

D.P.

When do they call the roll?
Midnight?

SNOWMAN

I'm no juist sure. Thon chappie
Wi' the hairy breist'll keep you right.
Oh! they do the thing no badly—
Singers an' a' laid on. . . .

D.P.

A Christmas tree—
I hadn't noticed. And presents too.
Who will they be for—
The guard,
The working squad that sweep the prison yard?

SNOWMAN

A wee bird

(*He signs to her to come closer.*)

Told me there was one for YOU!

D.P.

For me?

SNOWMAN

Noo,
No a word.
Dinna let dab. If onyone hears
That you've been tellt—
I micht as weel begin tae melt!

D.P.

But how did they know I'd come?

(*As she moves over to tree, she spots the doll's house and stops in wonder.*)

I think I know now
WHY I came. . . .

(*She runs to the tree picks up the toy and slowly carries it forward.*)

They've given me a HOME
As well as a name.

(*She puts it down and kneels beside it.*)

Oh, isn't it sweet!
Look—tiny doors
And curtains on the windows;
Red tiles on the roof,
A dear little cheeky chimney stack—
OH, I do love you so. . . .

My little house.
I'll have thick carpets on the floors. . . .
No
I'll stain the one in the hall!
And all
The rooms will glow with light,
The walls will be ever so
Ever so bright—
And hung with pictures.
I'll buy a grandfather clock
For the stairs. To treasure
And measure
The hours of pleasure and sweet content
This magical, make-believe night has sent.

(*The* MAN, *awakened by her shout of joy, has trailed down the rostrum steps with the toy donkey under his arm. He has stood as if yet another forgotten thing was seeping back into his memory. Now he steps forward and kneels at the other side of the doll's house. She doesn't look up until, after gazing silently awhile, he speaks. . . .*)

MAN

What is your name?

D.P.

I don't think I've got one. . . .
Unless it's 'The World'—
What's yours?

MAN

I haven't one either—
Unless it's 'The World'.

D.P.

Where have you come from?

MAN

I was asleep. . . .
But it can't have come yet.
My stocking was empty. And so is his.

D.P.

How strangely you speak.
What can't have come?

MAN

The midnight—
Oh! This is Neddy.

D.P.

How do you do?

MAN

He's my best friend.
We've been to the end
Of the world and back.
Sometimes he's a dragon
But sometimes that's me
And sometimes . . .
Would you like to play
Cowboys and Injuns?
Neddy, you see, isn't very like
An Injun, really.
Or, I don't mind:
Cops and robbers—if you'd rather.

D.P.

I'd rather
Not.
Thanks all the same,

But I've been playing a game
Like that ever since I can remember. . . .
I'd rather not. You play with me—
Look, I got this
From the Christmas tree. . . .

MAN

I think . . .

D.P.

There are curtains on the windows,
Red tiles on the roof—
Yes. . . .
What do you think?

MAN

I think . . . it's a very nice house.

D.P.

It looks quite real—
If only there was smoke
Coming from the chimney. . . .

MAN

I wanted to say . . . I think
I've seen those eyes before.
I couldn't forget. They're very beautiful.

D.P.

I have seen yours before.

MAN

Where? Tell me, where?

D.P.

I remember them looking at me
Over a gate. You were inside
And you locked it
When you saw me coming.
I sat down and cried. . . .

MAN

I don't remember a gate.

D.P.

I don't suppose you do.
Then once I saw you
At a rather imposing desk,
But you didn't bother that time
Even looking up.
You knew I was waiting, but you said
You couldn't see me,
Weren't to be disturbed.
You were too busy—and I could guess
The nature of your business.
You were busy . . .
Doodling
On a ground plan of the Heaven-upon-Earth,
Playing noughts and crosses
With yourself. Trimming your losses
Neatly back and sides.
Oh! You were wise—
I had nothing left to lose. . . .
The eyes
That were too busy to look up
Had everything.

45

MAN

If I'd only known you were there!
The numb-skulls can't have told me. . . .
Oh! I can look up now
And never wish an end to looking.
Look long,
And think I see there
All the dreams,
Every nightmare
Since the world began—in those eyes.
It's not too late to make amends
Is it too late to say we're friends?
We could both catch the midnight,
It will soon be here.

D.P.

There's the roll-call. No, I must be near
For that.

MAN

Is it too late?

(*There is a slight pause. Then she smiles.*)

Then,
Shall we *wait* . . . together?

(*They join hands and the one clasping still the doll's house and the other the donkey they pass beyond the Christmas tree and out of our sight. The* SINGERS *close the scene as they slowly approach from either side and, meeting centre stage, sing*):

This is the truth sent from above,
The truth of God, the God of love,
Therefore don't turn me from your door,
But hearken all both rich and poor.

46

The first thing which I do relate
Is that God did man create;
The next thing which to you I'll tell—
Woman was made with man to dwell.

And we were heir to endless woes,
Till God the Lord did interpose;
And so a promise soon did run
That he would redeem us by his Son.

Traditional

(*As the* SINGERS *leave the stage they pass the* SNOWMAN *who, with as gracious a gesture as his static girth will permit, doffs his bowler to them!*)

SNOWMAN

Weel . . . wonders'll never cease—
Looks like we'll hae a bit o' peace
At last.
The busiest nicht for mony winters past!
Hooses and donkeys and Christmas stockin's—
Never heard the like.
I doubt auld Santa's oot on strike,
I ken he doesna like folk peepin'—
Raither hae them sleepin'
When he comes.
Losh! Here's someone noo . . .
I wonder who—
I'd better pretend juist in case.

(*Loud and grossly exaggerated snores emanate from the* SNOWMAN, *as the* HERD *enters.*)

HERD

Asleep?

SNOWMAN

Eh? Oh, it's you. No. Juist doverin'.
There's been sic a thrang o' fowk hoverin'
It's quite worn me oot. . . .

HERD

Poor old world!

SNOWMAN

Noo, sir, dinna stert aa'
That world stuff on me.
See
Whaur it landed the others!
If I found that me and that cheeky wee brat
Who made fun o' my hat
Were brothers—
I'd . . . I'd gie up the ghost,
Ay, that's whit he cried me:
I'll gie him GHOST!
The most
We can be is first cousins.

HERD

But you *are* the world.
That's why you're here—
Perhaps it's why you're gone to-morrow.
The world that passes. . . .
Humanity, we might call *you*—
The flimsy, fleeting thing
That makes itself the laughing-stock
Of all Eternity
With its home-brewed self-importance.

Humanity—
Nailed down in a crate
And labelled 'FRAGILE'.
If only it would forget about the truth,
And stop to think
Which-side-up it finds itself,
Its worries would be over.
Humanity—
Rolled by God from pure unblemished
Drifts of Life,
And moulded in the semblance of a human kindness
All His own,
Set upon the highway of Creation
To seek its fortune.
And there set up,
Nothing is possible
But that Humanity grows grey
And dirty in the city smut.
Purity is forfeit in Creation—
The chief end
Of Humanity without a soul
Is the melting pot.

(*The* SNOWMAN *meanwhile has well and truly nodded off.*)

Asleep?

SNOWMAN

Eh? No. No. . . .
Weel mebbe juist dropped off the noo.
It's the fresh air set me noddin'.
Weel—
If I'm the world
It's no sic a bad place after a'.
But Guid kens whit'll happen
In the thaw,
An' aathing comes tae an end!

Friend,
Spare your sorrow
For the world tomorrow,
When the sun comes up
In his work-a-day way,
And the milk-boy dawn
Whistling over the hill
Gives the preening alarm-cock something new
To cock-a-doodle-do
About. When you see a new day
Just beginning,
And the lumbering roundabouts
Start their spinning,
Be sorry for the world
That has so soon forgotten
You and me,
The Christmas tree, and the midnight music.

But to-night. . . .
Quick. Wish yourself something
For your stocking.
While the midnight music's still in the air
Cast your wishing-net
On the snowy old ocean of your dreams.
Something always turns up, and
Your turn has come—
Think hard. . . . What is your wish?

SNOWMAN

To tell the truth I hadna thocht
I'd get a wish, or I'd hae been prepared.
Noo . . . let me see. . . .

(*He engages in some comic deliberation with himself.*)

A hoose, a donkey . . . ?
No, I was thinkin'—

An', that's no my line, as ye ken—
Gin it were somethin' wad gae ben
A stockin'. . . . Eh, haud it up . . . and let us see
It maun be somethin' wee. . . .
Noo whit wad fit?
Fit!
Man but that's it—the verra thing:
Fegs!
I wad like a pair o' legs!

HERD

Yours for the asking.

SNOWMAN

Mine for the stockin'!

HERD

What are you waiting for?
Come over here.

SNOWMAN

Noo sir, time enough to pu' my leg
When I've got ane!

HERD

Come over here. . . .

(*The* SNOWMAN *gives him a look of despair, then finds to his astonishment that he* CAN *move. He emerges from the prefabricated body—dressed in a white loose fitting jacket, baggy white trousers and huge black boots. His jacket has three big black buttons as had his body. He staggers slowly across the stage, at first like someone who is learning to walk—then with increasing confidence.*)

SNOWMAN

Guid sakes—they've come!
I can walk. Walk. D'ye see?
They feel as though . . . they belong tae me!
Noo I can rin an' dance an' a'—
An' wha gies a dockin' for the thaw
When he can rin and' dance an' a'.
Eh, whaur'll I can go to try them oot?

HERD

Round the world. You'll still
Be back in time—if you scoot.

SNOWMAN

In time? Oh, ay. . . .
Ye're sure I'll no melt
When I'm awa'—
The thaw
Will no catch up with me.

HERD

No, you won't melt, I'll guarantee—
Try striking a match, and then you'll see.

SNOWMAN

No match for me—
I've heard them say,
An' tae tell ye the truth I near had my day
Aaready the nicht.
I'll ne'er see the licht
Wi'oot takin' a scunner . . .
But . . . och, weel . . . I wonner. . . .

(*He feels in his pocket, and most improbably there is a box of matches there!*)

Here's some. . . . I'll try.

(He takes out the box of matches, holds a match at arm's length, strikes it and watches it burn up. Then very slowly indeed he brings it nearer and nearer to his face until it nearly scorches his nose!)

Man, ye're richt—I didna feel the wee-est tingle
That means I'll be able tae stan' at an ingle
An' warm my hurdies, an' never worry. . . .

HERD

You'll have to hurry.
Before the fading night
Goes altogether.

SNOWMAN

I'm aff.
Which is the wey roon' the warld?
And whit if I dinna win back?

HERD

You'll win all right.

SNOWMAN

Is it far?

HERD

As far as the surf on the farthest shore,
As far as the people who live next door
Or the beggar on the corner.
Near and far.
Over the hill and follow the Star!

(The SNOWMAN makes for the rostrum steps, finds great difficulty in

negotiating them for the first time—then he takes a deep breath, braces himself for the effort, and, with one tremendous rush, victory is his—and he is off! As the stage darkens to conceal the SNOWMAN'S BODY *which remains, the* HERD *makes his exit, the lamp above the other rostrum flickers into life and reveals the* SINGERS *who sing this carol of snow and mid-winter*):

In the bleak mid-winter,
   Frosty winds made moan,
Earth stood hard as iron,
   Water like a stone;
Snow had fallen, snow on snow,
   Snow on snow,
In the bleak mid-winter,
   Long ago.

Our God, heaven cannot hold Him,
   Nor earth sustain;
Heaven and earth shall flee away
   When He comes to reign:
In the bleak mid-winter
   A stable-place sufficed
The Lord God Almighty,
   Jesus Christ.

Angels and archangels
   May have gathered there,
Cherubim and seraphim
   Throngèd the air;
But His mother only,
   In her maiden bliss,
Worshipped the Belovèd
   With a kiss.

Christina Georgina Rossetti

(*'But his mother only'. . . . As we listen to these words we are conscious of the fact that a slight figure has entered and is now seated*

54

upon the bench on the other rostrum. Beside her is a well-worn shopping
basket filled to overflowing with household articles and provisions—
a bunch of black grapes and a long loaf of bread protrude precariously.
She is now with obvious relish taking off her outdoor shoes and putting
on her slippers. They are very old and very comfortable.)

MOTHER

Christmas!
Sometimes I think in many ways
I'll be glad when it's over,
And there are three-hundred shopping days
Between me and the next one.
And yet,
I don't really mind
All the worry and rush—
It's worth it for the scurrying crush
Of good intention
Everywhere.
The baking and the queuing,
Making and doing,
They're all part of Christmas,
The wonder and joy. . . .
The peace and goodwill bit,
It
Matters the most to me.
I suppose I could thole all the queues
In the world—like my shoes,
At a pinch
For that: A little peace!
A little peace goes a long way
To making the most of our midnight,
And where there's goodwill
There's a way to set right
The wrong
That we've done through the day.
But the day is so long—
And the midnight flies so quickly. . . .

(She rises, moves down the steps of the rostrum, pauses a moment by the Christmas tree, and leaves there her basket. She has moved from the light of the lamp, and the stage is dark and quiet. 'Eerie' might describe it for others—to her there is something of the softness of twilight in the shadows. She sits.)

No one about.
How silent and still
The suffering can be
And the travail. . . .
A sea of pity
And only the echo of its sighing
From tiny shells lying
In the shingle.
I have known the agonies
Of seedtime and harvest,
The whither whimsy of the moon,
The pain of loving
With more love than the stars
Falling late and soon
Can comprehend.
The end
Of my loving is Creation's end.
I am a mother,
And the world in me knows
The littleness of its beginning.
Surely it remembers
Sometimes
The care that cradled it,
The fondling eyes that watched it grow—
And saw it go
In a fullness of time
And an emptiness of grief.
There they go my children. . . .
My hopes and dreams,
My longings—
There they go. . . .
Small specks on the horizon now,

Now no more. . . .
The candle in the window
The watching and the waiting . . . all that's left.
The waiting—
That's the thing that makes
The living possible.
There's always something worth
The waiting for.
How the world in me waits. . . .
How the loving in me waits. . . .
How the mother in me waits. . . .

(*Now are the interminable moments of waiting. There is not a
movement. The* MOTHER *sits on among the shadows; the* SINGERS
*have never left the rostrum. Their voices creep to her through the
darkness—perhaps they never quite reach her. . . .*)

I sing of a maiden
    That is makèless;
King of all kinges
    To her son she ches.

He came all so stille
    Where his mother was,
As dew in Aprille
    That falleth on the grass.

He came all so stille
    To his mother's bowr,
As dew in Aprille
    That falleth on the flower.

He came all so stille
    Where his mother lay,
As dew in Aprille
    That falleth on the spray.

Mother and maiden
　　Was never none but she;
Well may such a lady
　　Godès mother be.

15th Century

(*The* HERD *comes out of the shadows, but the* MOTHER *does not look up. She is at first aware only of a presence. . . .*)

MOTHER

Is *my* waiting long?

HERD

No. Not now.

MOTHER

Will they come back?

HERD

Yes, they'll come back.

MOTHER

And will they remember—
Or is it too long?

HERD

They'll remember.

MOTHER

My children. . . .
Where have they been?

HERD

Near and far.

MOTHER

Have they been waiting too?

HERD

Yes, for the midnight. Waiting too.

MOTHER

What of *her* child? . . .
Will He come back?
Will He remember, do you think?

HERD

The children of the world
Won't let Him come back.
His waiting will be long. . . .
But He'll remember.

MOTHER

What will they call her child?

HERD

The Son of Man will be His name,
And the Christmas Tree
That bears His love
Will bear our shame.

MOTHER

When will that be?

HERD

When your children
Turn their back on love,
Forget the giving
In the living,
Weave for Him a Crown of Scorns
And laugh at His forgiveness.

MOTHER

And what of her?
Where will she be then?

HERD

Waiting still. . . .

MOTHER

There is no waiting
Like a Mother's—
Filled with wondering and fears.

HERD

Unless *my* waiting—
Endless through all the ages.

MOTHER

Who are you? I seem to know
Your voice. Come out of the shadows.
Let me look at you.

HERD

I was your child once
In the long ago—

But now I am an orphan
Of time and space
Without a place
In the reckonings of reason,
An angel, you might call me,
Out of season,
Till the season of my Master's
Joy and Peace is born.
Don't look so forlorn!
Mother-that-was, my wondrous tale is told!

MOTHER

But, laddie, you'll catch your death of cold
Running through time and space
Half naked!

HERD

Mother-that-*was*—I said.
Come, sit here in the place of honour.
I hear your children coming.
Quickly . . . that's right.

MOTHER

Oh, am I an awful sight?
Is my hair quite tidy? Oh, and
Where did I put my basket?
There. Are they coming? I'm ready.

(The HERD *takes the silk kerchief from the tree and gently blindfolds her. . . .*)

Here, what are you doing?
I can't see a thing. . . .
Is it blind-man's buff?
That's long enough. One, two, three . . .
What's happening?

(As she protests in a good-humoured way, on to the stage come creeping the MAN, *the* DISPLACED PERSON, *followed by the* SNOWMAN *who in all his travels has developed a corn! They creep round her and see that she is blindfolded. One by one they kneel before her.)*

D.P.

Hello, Mother.

MOTHER

My child, my little one.
You have come back to me.

D.P.

I have come for the roll-call.

MOTHER

What roll-call, my sweet?

D.P.

They put me in prison.
I didn't belong—
And there's a punishment for not belonging.

MOTHER

But you are the world, pet,
You belong to me.
I'll speak to them.

D.P.

They don't listen
When you speak to them—
There's too much to do to listen.

MOTHER

Your hands are rough. . . .
What have they made you do?
Your knuckles are bruised. . . .

D.P.

They made me knock
At all the doors—
But no one would answer,
They were all too busy.
My heart too is bruised.
But it's all right now, mother.
I've found a home at last—
With curtains on the windows and . . .
Now I belong.

MAN

Hello Mother.

MOTHER

I know that voice. Hello, my child.
Did you find the fortune
You set out to seek. You'll be famous now,
And important too.
What has fortune brought to you, my son?

MAN

I grew up too quickly—
And forgot how to laugh—
There's not much to laugh about, really.
I got out of the way,
And well, when there's no laughter
Not long after
You've got to fight
For survival.

MOTHER

You've not been fighting!
What in the world was there to fight
About?

MAN

Nothing IN the world at all, Mother,
This and that—
The world itself is the root
Of the trouble.

MOTHER

And you are the world, my son.
Oh, why must you fight!

MAN

It's according to plan,
And planning's my life—
Or at least it was,
Until I got scared, and ran
For my life.
I thought I might miss the Midnight home.

SNOWMAN

Hello, Mother.

MOTHER

And you, my child,
You have come back—
I was most afraid for you.
Have they told you how long?
It seems so short. . . .
And so lonely. . . . If only
Your world could remain.

SNOWMAN

To tell the truth, Mother,
I'm glad that it doesna'.
It's hard work tae keep
My soul clean as it is.
I'd hae tae stert thinkin'—
An' thoughts are gey queer.
I'd near
Be as well as I am.
I've seen a' the sichts—
An' their tropical nichts
Leave me as cold as before.

MOTHER

My busy, wandering, fleeting dreams,
My labour, my suckling, and my joy,
My loving and living,
My finding, my giving,
My waking, my sleeping,
My taking, my keeping. . . .
My children.
Where is my lost child?
Won't you come back?

HERD

(who has been standing by himself, and is much moved.)

There's no going back
Ever.
In time and space and reason,
In the season
Of the coming of my King
There's no going back.
My task
To take the bandage from the world's eyes

That it may gaze at Midnight
On the Miracle of Love,
See the Joy, the Peace, the Glory
Sent it from above.

(*He unties the kerchief from the* MOTHER'S *eyes, and as he does so the
first stroke of midnight reverberates through the air. As moved by
some instinctive impulse, the five kneel facing the Christmas tree, the
 HERD in the middle; and the* SINGERS *process to each striking of the
hour, taking their place on either side of the tree. When the last hour
strikes, all are in position. Very gradually the Star of the Tree lights
from within, and through the silver gauze we see, framed in the cut-out
shape of the star, Mary, the Mother of Christ, with the Holy Infant
in her arms. While we gaze, with the others, in wonder, the* SINGERS
sing this tender lullaby):

Lullay my liking, my dear son, my sweeting;
Lullay my dear heart, mine own dear darling!

I saw a fair maiden
    Sitten and sing:
She lulled a little child,
    A sweete lording:

That eternal lord is he
    That made alle thing;
Of alle lordes he is Lord,
    Of alle kinges king:

There was mickle melody
    At that childes birth:
Although they were in heaven's bliss
    They made mickle mirth:

Angels bright they sang that night
    And saiden to that child
'Blessed be thou, and so be she
    That is both meek and mild':

66

Pray we now to that child,
    And to his mother dear,
God grant them all his blessing
    That now maken cheer.

15th Century

(*By the last verse of this carol, the only light is that which spills to the front stage from the Crib Scene in the star and silhouettes the kneeling figures. In turn they bring their gifts to the Christmas tree. . . .*)

SNOWMAN

Haly Bairn
I bring tae Thee
The mantlin' o' Humanitie:
The flowin' tide, the fleein' hour,
The settin' sun, the fadin' flower.
The sword o' strife, the breath o' life,
Humanitie I bring tae Thee,
Haly Bairn o' Charitie.

D.P.

Holy Stranger
With a manger
For your bed.
House-room in the world
I bring
As my humble offering.
Room for Peace,
Displaced, neglected,
Room for Love,
Despised, rejected,
Holy stranger
With a manger
For your bed.

Infant King,
Star of the East,
To thee I bring
This gentle beast
To bear Thee on Thy Royal Way,
To bear Thee on Thy Triumph Day
When the banners are unfurled
And Thy Glory through the world
Streams like shafts of summer light.
Through the darkest gloom of night,
Noon-bright Sun,
Thy will be done. . . .
Infant King,
Star of the East,
To Thee I bring
This gentle beast.

MOTHER

Little Jesus,
Saviour of the world Thou art,
Lamb of God,
Child of my heart.
Wine-grapes and bread
To Thee I bring
To be for a remembering
Until Thy Kingdom come.

SINGERS

Now the holly bears a berry as white as the milk,
And Mary bore Jesus, who was wrapped up in silk:

And Mary bore Jesus Christ our Saviour for to be,
And the first tree in the greenwood, it was the holly,
   holly! holly!
And the first tree in the greenwood, it was the holly.

Now the holly bears a berry as green as the grass,
And Mary bore Jesus Christ, who died on the cross:

Now the holly bears a berry as black as the coal,
And Mary bore Jesus, who died for us all:

Now the holly bears a berry, as blood is it red,
Then trust we our Saviour, who rose from the dead.

Sans Day Carol: Cornish

(The Crib Scene fades from our sight. . . . The lamps of the world are alight once more, and bring back the oh! so familiar colours and shadows of everyday living. For a moment it seems the spell will remain unbroken, then each in turn rises. The MOTHER *takes up her basket and moves up to the rostrum bench where she sits to put on her out-door shoes again; the* DISPLACED PERSON *takes up her bundle, the* MAN *his brief-case, his umbrella, and his bowler hat; the* SNOWMAN *totters back to the body which he left. The four exit severally. At the foot of the Christmas tree are now the toy donkey, the doll's house, the silk kerchief, as at the beginning.*

The SINGERS *rise, and, singing, they process slowly to the front of the stage and by proscenium steps down into the auditorium itself, and through the audience, until their voices are lost in the world beyond— these words still on their lips):*

O come, all ye faithful,
Joyful and triumphant,
Come ye, O come ye to Bethlehem;
Come and behold Him
Born the King of angels:
O come, let us adore Him, Christ the Lord.

Sing, choirs of angels,
Sing in exultation,
Sing, all ye citizens of heaven above,
Glory to God
In the highest:
O come, let us adore Him, Christ the Lord.

Yea, Lord, we greet Thee,
Born this happy morning;
Jesus, to Thee be glory given,
Word of the Father,
Now in flesh appearing:
O come, let us adore Him, Christ the Lord.

18th Century:
Translated by Frederick Oakley

(*The* HERD *alone is left, where still he kneels....*)

HERD

So soon...
The midnight fades,
The angel-song is stilled,
And Earth filled
With a miracle
Of forgetting.
The back-shifting world
Has 'Business as Usual'
On its door. Goes back
To more
Wandering and futility.
Lays by
The patience and humility
Of the midnight waiting.
One by one
The stars blow out,
And Wise Men turn about
For home,
Shepherds take
The old drove-roads
Across the hill to market.
Gone
The moment of magic.
It is finished. Nothing left...
But to forget.

Yet
Every eve of every year—
Is Christmas Eve.
God's is the waiting;
The Son,
Stirring in the hearts of men,
Leaping in the Womb of Time,
Waits. . . .
Waits for the Earth
To give Him birth,
And human choirs
To sing His coming.
Wake, sleeping world,
And sing!
This Holy Christmas
Is a thing
For the remembering!

(The lights fade—for a moment the stage is in utter, desolate darkness, and then a shaft of light from above reveals the HERD *sitting where first we saw him at the opening of the play. It is essentially the first scene re-created. . . .)*

Every eve of every year
Alone
And unattended by the world
I sit here.
Sit upon this upland waste of Time
Piping a tune to the singing-silvered spheres;
The theme Eternal—
Of a Will and Purpose
Over and above all things;
Above all, good;
The theme Eternal
Born into flesh and blood,
Conceived above,
Born into agony and love.

(*Picking up his shepherd's pipe, he starts to play. The little tune has a tender, persistent appeal. We have heard it before.*

'*It is as if he sat there for ever, playing to the night sky. . . .*'

The solitary shaft of light fades, and there is only a timeless music floating to us from the darkness, as the curtain falls.)

THE END

0/x